Jerry Spinelli

The Library of Author Biographies™

JERRY SPINELLI

David Seidman

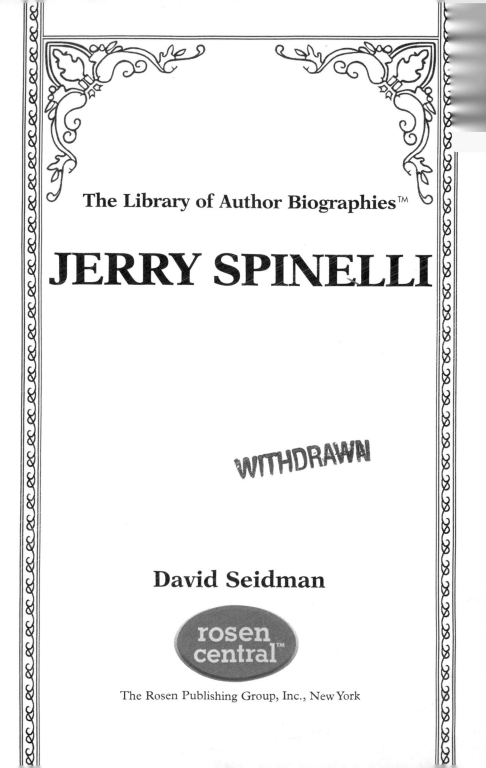

rosen central™

The Rosen Publishing Group, Inc., New York

To David and Bobbi Weiss, who understand the writer's life

Published in 2004 by The Rosen Publishing Group, Inc.
29 East 21st Street, New York, NY 10010

Library of Congress Cataloging-in-Publication Data

Seidman, David, 1959–
Jerry Spinelli / David Seidman.— 1st ed.
   p. cm. — (The library of author biographies)
Summary: Discusses life and work of the popular children's author, including his writing process and methods, inspirations, a critical discussion of his books, biographical timeline, and awards. Includes bibliographical references and index.
ISBN 0-8239-4016-0 (lib. bdg.)
1. Spinelli, Jerry—Juvenile literature. 2. Authors, American—20th century—Biography—Juvenile literature. 3. Children's stories—Authorship—Juvenile literature. [1. Spinelli, Jerry. 2. Authors, American. 3. Authorship.] I. Title. II. Series.
PS3569.P546Z87 2003
813'.54—dc21

         2002156615

Manufactured in the United States of America

Text from *Jason and Marceline* by Jerry Spinelli. Copyright © 1986 by Jerry Spinelli. By permission of Little, Brown and Company, Inc.

Text from *Knots in My Yo-Yo String* by Jerry Spinelli. Copyright © 1998 by Jerry Spinelli. Used by permission of Random House Children's Books, a division of Random House, Inc.

Text from *Maniac Magee* by Jerry Spinelli. Copyright © 1989 by Jerry Spinelli. By permission of Little, Brown and Company, Inc.

Text from *Night of the Whale* by Jerry Spinelli, pp. 19–20. Copyright © 1985 by Jerry Spinelli. By permission of Little, Brown and Company, Inc.

Text from *Space Station Seventh Grade* by Jerry Spinelli. Copyright © 1982 by Jerry Spinelli. By permission of Little, Brown and Company, Inc.

Text from *Tooter Pepperday* by Jerry Spinelli. Copyright © 1995 by Jerry Spinelli. Used by permission of Random House Children's Books, a division of Random House, Inc.

Table of Contents

Introduction: The Successful Failure

Jerry Spinelli told himself, "Man, I'm failing like a champ."[1] He had spent more than a decade writing novels, but publishers had rejected them all. His life was not all that bad, though. He was happily married and enjoyed being the stepfather to his wife's children. In fact, one of his kids was about to change his life.

One night, after the family had chicken for dinner, Spinelli put the leftovers in a paper bag. The next morning, he took them to work. At lunchtime, he closed his office door to eat and, as he usually did at lunch, work on a novel. He opened the bag and, to his surprise, he found a bunch of bones. Spinelli realized that one of his children must have sneaked to the fridge, eaten the chicken, and slipped the bones back into the lunch bag.

Spinelli knew a funny situation when he saw one. He started to write it up as a scene in a novel about adults with adult problems, just like his other novels. But then it hit him: Write the story from the viewpoint of the chicken-eating kid.

> One by one my stepfather took the chicken bones out of the bag and laid them on the kitchen table. He laid them down real neat. In a row. Five of them. Two leg bones, two wing bones, one thigh bone.
>
> And bones is all they were. There wasn't a speck of meat on them.
>
> Was this really happening? Did my stepfather really drag me out of bed at seven o'clock in the morning on my summer vacation so I could stand in the kitchen in my underpants and stare down at a row of chicken bones?[2]

What Jerry Spinelli wrote would become *Space Station Second Grade* (1981), his first children's book. From then on, he would write books about kids and teenagers, books that would earn him awards and thousands of fans.

But getting to that point took a long time and a meandering path.

1 Beginnings

"The first 15 years of my life turned out to be one long research project," Jerry Spinelli told a reporter in an interview he gave in 2001. "I thought I was merely growing up in Norristown, Pennsylvania. Looking back now, I can see that all the time, I was gathering material that would one day find its way into my books."[1]

It started with Spinelli's grandfather, Italian orphan Alessandro "Alex" Spinelli. In 1900, when Alex was fourteen, his adopted family sent him to the United States, where he became a laborer for the Pennsylvania Department of Highways. He never fully mastered English, but he made an impact on his grandson. Spinelli's best-known novel, *Maniac Magee* (1990), tells how an old man left home at age fifteen, didn't learn to read or write English, became a laborer for local schools and parks, and befriended an eleven-year-old boy.

In 1909, after settling in the small southeast Pennsylvania city of Norristown, Alex and his wife, Millie, had a son, Louis. In 1933, Louis was at a dance at the Orioles Lodge (the meeting place of a local service organization) when he spotted Lorna Bigler. With her shapely legs, wide smile, and dark, curly hair, Lorna was striking. Louis said to his friend Babe Richards, "See that girl. That's who I'm going to marry."[2]

On May 16, 1936, the two wed. On February 1, 1941, their first child was born. They named him Jerry.

Spinelli's First Books

"Most writers were reading *Little Women* [Louisa May Alcott; 1869] when they were six years old," Spinelli told a journalist in 1999. "I had a subscription to *Bugs Bunny* comics."[3] Not that anything stopped him from reading *Little Women* or any other book. "Some of my earliest memories are of my mother reading to me, stories like [Jean de Brunhoff's] *Babar* and [Watty Piper's] *The Little Engine That Could*. My parents steered me in the right direction."[4]

Still, books weren't important to young Jerry: "I read maybe ten of them, fifteen tops, from the day I entered first grade until graduation from high school."[5] Mostly, though, Jerry read comic books—lots of them. In addition to *Bugs Bunny*, he read cowboy and war comics. And he followed the columns of Red McCarthy, sports editor at the Norristown *Times Herald*. As Spinelli would later say, "Until then I had thought there was only one English language—the language I spoke and heard in the West End of Norristown. I was happily surprised to discover that there was more than one way to say something, that the words and their arrangement could be as interesting as the thing they said."[6]

But that was about it. "I regret that I did not read and write more as a kid,"[7] Spinelli said years later. "When I did read, I enjoyed it, but when I thought about how to spend my spare time, reading didn't usually come to mind. Baseball, football, and basketball did."[8]

The Good Sport

Jerry had always liked sports, but in fifth grade, he became a serious player. "No longer were my seasons summer, fall, winter, and spring but baseball, football, and basketball. I was a sports nut,"[9] he wrote. He later commented, "I was raised practically in a locker room."[10]

And he did well. He was the fifty-yard-dash (forty-six meter) champion of Norristown grade schools. At age eleven, he started playing Biddy Baseball, the local version of Little League, and became a top shortstop. By the time he hit high school, Jerry knew his destiny: shortstop for baseball's royalty, the New York Yankees.

"I think some of that [sports experience] I've simply used in my books,"[11] Spinelli said years later. In *Maniac Magee*, the homeless main character Jeffrey "Maniac" Magee becomes a hero for hitting home runs off a pitcher who strikes out everyone else. In *There's a Girl in My Hammerlock* (1991), teenage Maisie Potter earns fame and enemies by joining a boy's wrestling team. In *Crash* (1996), the tough and bullying John "Crash" Coogan is a star athlete who, in the book's most important event, loses a crucial race. And a good deal of *Who Ran My Underwear Up the*

Flagpole? (1992) involves Eddie Mott, a middle school football player.

A Passion for Perfection

Jerry's skill at sports didn't come from raw aggression, enormous size, or cobra-strike quickness. According to Spinelli, in Biddy Baseball, "I made the all-star team . . . as much for what I did not do as for what I did. That is to say, I did not make mistakes."[12]

He was just as devoted to flawlessness off the field. He was neat, tidy, and organized. He always obeyed rules, and not once did he have to stay after school for detention. Instead, he was handed chores that schoolteachers call honors, like raising the school's flags. What's more, he "attended First Presbyterian Church nearly every Sunday." As he says, "I had a little ladder of attendance medals that I wore proudly on my sport coat."[13]

Jerry's need to avoid sloppiness or wildness muffled his urges and drives. By junior high school, he was very quiet and rarely even laughed out loud.

Something was bubbling up inside him, though. It was "the urge to write a poem, to daydream, to ruminate, to wonder . . . I swooned just thinking about things," he recalled. "Like space. I tried to imagine, tried to grasp the speed of light. One hundred eighty-six thousand miles per *second!* And how about those stars up there? . . . I tried to imagine zooming out past the last stars and looking around—at what? What does the end of the universe look like?"[14] Thoughts like that, which stretched Jerry's imagination, were good training for a writer.

Race

When Jerry did do anything unusual, he did it quietly. At first, he may not have even realized that he was doing anything different at all.

Like many American towns in the 1940s and 1950s, Norristown was firmly divided. African Americans lived on the East Side and whites like Jerry on the West Side. The two groups rarely mingled. But after Jerry became an athlete at age ten, he broke the color line. As he put it, "[Blacks] ceased to be black and I ceased to be white. Instead we were teammates or opponents, identified by the color of our uniforms, not of our skin."[15]

The problems of dealing with the racial divide became a main theme in *Maniac Magee*.

Like Jerry, Maniac doesn't fight racism as much as he simply doesn't understand it.

Tough Guy

But Jerry did understand one thing: a hunger for violence. Like many obedient boys, Jerry sometimes wondered if he was a wimp. That concern hit especially hard around sixth grade, as he watched playground fights. "I saw other kids flailing and clubbing, tearing each other's shirts to shreds, trading bloody noses, and I said to myself, 'Hey, why not me?'"[16] He turned this urge into a fight with a small, skinny kid named Joey Stackhouse, as he recounted in his 1998 autobiography, *Knots in My Yo-Yo String.*

I convinced myself that [he] was asking for it . . .

I balled my fist and swung . . . A punch has a double impact, as I was about to learn, and only the first lands on the chin. Joey's eyes widened. He stood there staring at me with such wild astonishment that I knew at once he had not, not in a million years, been asking for it. He started to cry. He blurted out, "Why'd you do that?" and ran back down George Street.

If ever I had notions of becoming a warrior, they died that day.[17]

Best of the Best

The Stackhouse fight was an exception. As he slipped from childhood to adolescence, Jerry continued to be a good boy. He didn't even fight very much with his younger brother, Bill, born in 1945.

The peak of his perfection came as ninth grade—and junior high school—slid to an end. "I was one of those kids with a couple inches of activities under my name in the yearbook," he said. "In junior high, I played football, basketball, and baseball. Besides being valedictorian, I was class president and king of the prom (my girlfriend was queen). And I was voted 'most popular boy.'"[18]

Afterward, though, things got hard.

2 The Downward Slide

A fan once asked Jerry Spinelli, "What was your greatest difficulty growing up?" He answered, "Going from being such a big shot in junior high to a 'nobody' in my first year of high school."[1]

One of Jerry's problems was schoolwork. He liked some of his classes—English, appropriately for a writer-to-be, was a favorite—but he hit trouble elsewhere. "Whereas I had been a ninth-grade whiz at algebra, geometry in tenth grade befuddled me,"[2] he explained. "I just couldn't seem to picture dimensions in my head."[3]

He ran into emotional difficulties, too. As he later says, "I do recall at times being possessive and picky and unreasonable and immature."[4] In addition, Jerry knew dread. "Every February 1— the date of my birth—prodded me closer to the ominous cloud that hung over my future. It was called the draft, and it meant that when I (and all other boys deemed healthy enough) got out of high school or college, I would have to join the armed forces,"[5] he wrote later.

What's more, Jerry lost his home. For ten years, he had lived in a safe, familiar house. But then his family moved to a different part of town. "Dismal. Dreary. Gray. These are the words that come to mind when I think of that time,"[6] he remembered.

Worst of all, Jerry had to face an ugly fact: He wasn't going to be a professional athlete. The former fifty-yard-dash champion lost his speed. He wasn't developing the bulk of a football champion or the height of a basketball star. In baseball, "I had no equal when it came to standing at shortstop and chattering to my pitcher: 'C'mon, baby, hum the pea.' Unfortunately, when I stood at the plate, so many peas were hummed past me for strikes that I decided to let somebody else become shortstop for the Yankees."[7]

Luckily, he found another calling.

Goal to Go

In 1957, Jerry watched his beloved high school football team, the Norristown Eagles, pull a shocking last-minute victory over a power-ful rival team. Jerry was thrilled, but he had a problem. He wrote:

> No matter how many times I replayed the goal-line stand in my head, I kept falling short of satisfaction. The scoreboard had said the game was over, but for me it wasn't . . .
>
> And then for no reason that I can recall, I sat down at my study desk and reached for a pencil and paper and wrote down a title.[8]

The title was "Goal to Go." Under it, Jerry wrote a poem that began, "The score stood 7–6, With but five minutes left to go." He ended it with "But when the dust had cleared the fight, the Eagle line had held."[9] "It's as though that goal-line stand did not totally happen until I wrote the poem about it," Spinelli said. "Then bam, the experience was over."[10]

But it wasn't. Jerry gave "Goal to Go" to his father, a passionate Norristown High sports fan. A few days later, he opened the *Times Herald*'s sports section and to his shock found his poem there. And the following day at school, everyone told him how much they enjoyed the piece.

And after that, Jerry began to think of himself as a writer. Even after he and his books became famous, Spinelli kept a framed *Times Herald* clipping of the poem hanging above his desk.

He soon found out that getting published wouldn't always be so easy.

3 Writing and Rejection

When Jerry Spinelli graduated from high school, he was old enough to be drafted. At that time, a draft-age male who went to college could get a student deferment—a paper that kept you out of the draft. That, apparently, was Jerry's situation. He went to Gettysburg College, a school of about three thousand students approximately 100 miles (160 kilometers) west of Norristown.

Spinelli hasn't spoken much about his first days after Norristown High. However, in his novel *Night of the Whale* (1985), the narrator is a would-be writer who has just graduated from high school. Warren "Mouse" Umlau plans to attend Dickinson College, not far from Gettysburg. Mouse, possibly like Jerry himself, isn't sure that he's ready for college life. As he says:

> Where was I when they handed out appetites and stamina? I wanted to have a total college experience, but I didn't seem to have the tools. What would I do at a party—say, "Excuse me, it's eleven o'clock, I have to go to bed"? Or, "Do you have any smaller beer cans? This one's too big." I was supposedly going to college to study journalism, but if someone had handed me an application form right then, under Career Choice I would have put "Drinker of Gallons."[1]

Rejection

At Gettysburg, Spinelli majored in English. He may have thought of himself as a writer, but he was a long way from becoming one. "Nobody told me how hard it was going to be," he explained years later. "Lugging a pencil across the paper was sometimes harder than lugging 100-pound bags of concrete."[2]

His hard work got him nowhere. He wrote short stories and sent them to publishers—and they sent him rejection slips and refused to print the stories. "I began to write short stories, send them out, and begin my impressive collection of rejection slips,"[3] he said. Nonetheless, Spinelli didn't quit. As he said, "I discovered that even after a day of rejection slips, the sun comes up [the] next morning. And the stories were still in me. How could I not write?"[4]

Aside from this comment, Spinelli has rarely talked publicly about his college years. He's mentioned that he worked one summer as a psychiatric aide at Norristown State Hospital. He also taught college composition for a semester but didn't like the job's pickier aspects. "I really didn't care that much about comma placement and things like that," he said later. "I cared about [the students'] ability to express themselves and how well they were writing."[5]

Spinelli graduated from Gettysburg in 1963 and went on to postgraduate studies at Johns Hopkins University in Baltimore, Maryland (about fifty miles [eighty kilometers] southeast of Gettysburg), to take the school's writing seminars. According to Johns Hopkins' Web site, writing seminar students devote a year to writing and studying "with the aim of becoming published authors soon after graduation."[6]

Into the World

Spinelli completed the course, but before he could conquer the publishing world, he had to face Uncle Sam. As he recalls, in 1965, "Rather than wait to be drafted, I signed up for the Naval Air Reserve [and] went to boot camp in Memphis and photographic intelligence school in Denver."[7] A reservist—a part-time serviceman who receives training and returns to civilian life, where he keeps himself available in case the government needs extra troops—usually trains one weekend a month, plus a two-week stretch every year for up to eight years.

Since reserve service didn't pay much, Spinelli needed a regular job. In 1966, he worked as an editor for a magazine that went to department stores. He didn't like it. "When I went out into the working world with the three-piece-suit type of people, I wasn't talking like them; I was still back in the locker room,"[8] he said. But the real problem, as he would say, was that "it was an exciting, even glamorous job for somebody, but not me. I needed a job that would let me go at five o'clock, that would leave me with energy and time to do my own writing. I needed a boring job."[9]

He got one. The Chilton Company of Radnor, Pennsylvania, less than ten miles (sixteen kilometers) south of Norristown, published business magazines like *Food Engineering International* and *Instruments & Control Systems*.

As Spinelli laughingly told an interviewer, when "Chilton hired me as an editor, I told the secretary I was writing a book, so I would only be there a year or two. That turned into 23."[10]

Over the next three years, Spinelli spent his spare time—weekends, lunchtimes, nights—writing a novel. No publisher wanted it. Still, he was making some progress. "Back in 1966, I began jotting down notes about an unusual person,"[11] he told an interviewer. The notes would turn into Stargirl Caraway, the lead character of one of Spinelli's most popular books, *Stargirl* (2000). At the time, though, the story didn't work. After one hundred pages, Spinelli put it aside.

His Own Stargirl

Although Spinelli had problems with writing, his personal life was blooming. In the mid-1960s, he met Eileen Mesi. She was a secretary at Chilton and, like Spinelli, an aspiring writer. He remembered: "I first became aware of Eileen's presence in the world when I came in to work one day and found a chocolate Easter bunny at my desk."[12] Eileen had left it there. But Spinelli didn't get to know her until, as he says, "we bumped into each other at the trolley . . . Eileen had—as she always did in those days—three or four looseleaf binders stuffed with her poetry, and she shoved them into my arms and made me read them while we waited for the train. For some reason, she was impressed that I was an editor at the magazine where we both worked."[13]

The two became friends. Eileen was about a year younger than Spinelli and had grown up in Pennsylvania less than twenty miles (thirty-two kilometers) south of Norristown. She had been writing poetry since childhood but had published very little. During the next several years, Eileen and Spinelli showed each other their work and sympathized with each other when publishers rejected it.

Spinelli has said that Eileen is a real-life Stargirl. In the novel, quiet high school student Leo Borlock falls in love with Stargirl and says, "She taught me to revel [celebrate]. She taught me to wonder. She taught me to laugh. My sense of humor had always measured up to everyone else's; but timid, introverted me, I showed it sparingly: I was a smiler. In her presence, I threw back my head and laughed out loud for the first time in my life."[14] It's likely that Jerry Spinelli felt the same way about Eileen Mesi.

In the late 1960s, throughout the 1970s, and into the 1980s, Spinelli slipped into a routine:

writing novels, four of them in all, and having them rejected. He thinks of what he calls "those four failures" as "exercises that helped [him] learn how to write."[15] In addition, on May 21, 1977, Eileen and Spinelli got married. "Boy, did I get married!"[16] he said. Eileen already had several children.

Raising them was hard. "In the early days of Jerry and Eileen's marriage . . . money was tight,"[17] said John Keller, Spinelli's publisher. As Spinelli himself put it, "For years . . . we survived on thrift shops, yard sales, and double coupons."[18]

Around the start of the 1980s, Spinelli discovered the leftover gnawed chicken bones that one of the children had put in his lunch bag. "When I discovered the chicken was gone," he wrote later, "I did what I had done after the big football victory [in high school]: I wrote about it."[19]

That act would change his life.

4 The Upward Struggle

When asked where he got his ideas for his writing, Spinelli once said, "For my first two books, I didn't even have to look outside my own house."[1] And for his book *Space Station Seventh Grade*, he relied on a mixture of memory and imagination.

The story—a year in the life of a young man, Jason Herkimer—is actually several tales, set in the fictional town of Avon Oaks, Pennsylvania. Just as Spinelli felt lost and confused when he first entered high school, Jason runs into troubles when he moves from elementary school to junior high:

> The first week of school is over. I hated it. I'm not going back.

I wish I was back in the sixth grade. I was important there. I'm nothing here . . .

I had to go to the bathroom. The door didn't say Young Men. It said Boys. As soon as I opened it a ninth-grader took a cigarette out of his mouth and said, "Watta you lookin' at, faggot-face?" I walked out.[2]

Another aspect of Spinelli that went into the character of Jason is the desire to ponder the cosmos. It appears in *Space Station*'s "Grandmothers," which Spinelli has called his favorite chapter in all of his books. It involves a conversation between Jason and his friend Peter.

We both thought about [the man-made satellite] *Pioneer* for a while. Out there. Sailing through space . . .

"Know what really gets me?" [I asked.]

"What?"

I closed my eyes, said it slow. "When I think . . . of *Pioneer* . . . going . . . out . . . past . . . Pluto. Know what I mean?"

"Yeah. I know."

"It passes Pluto . . . and it's *out* . . . of the Solar System. *Out* of it. Heading . . . heading . . ."

I looked at my arm. "Peter, look! My arm! See?"

They were there, all over my arm: goosebumps.[3]

The book took about six months to write. But could Spinelli get a publisher to buy it? Fortunately, he didn't have to sell it himself. The book business is full of literary agents who do that job. He found one, but the agent took nearly a year to sell the book.

"I first came upon Jerry's work sometime in 1981, when a manuscript by a writer I'd never heard of from an agent I didn't know landed on my desk," said John Keller, publisher at Little, Brown and Company. "When I began to read, I liked the first chapter's conversational, unpretentious tone. It wasn't, however, until I got to the fourth chapter, 'Hair,' that I knew I had happened upon a writer who was special. When I read that chapter, in which Jason Herkimer tells about his ambivalent feelings about the onset of puberty and the absence or presence of pubic hair as noted in the boy's shower room after gym class, I broke into a big grin and thought, Exactly!"[4]

This is what Keller was referring to.

I'm thinking about hair all the time these days. All I have to do is hear somebody say the word and I start laughing. The same thing is happening to [my friend] Richie and a lot of other guys.

At first I thought it was just me. It started the first time we had to get a shower after gym class . . .

Hair. That was the first thing I noticed. Joe Sorbito had pubic hair. Lots of it.

What's funny is, Joe Sorbito is little. He's one of the littlest guys in seventh grade. And he's not older than anybody else either. He just has hair. It's a weird feeling being in the same shower with him, especially if it happens to be just the two of you. It's like I thought he was like me but I found out he's not. It makes you feel like a little kid again.[5]

"That, I believe, is Jerry's greatest strength," Keller concluded. "He gets it right."[6]

Space Station was published in 1982 to mixed reviews. "Spinelli has produced a first-rate story,"[7] said a reviewer from *Voice of Youth Advocates*, a librarians' magazine. A writer in the book-review publication *Kirkus Reviews* called it "consistently zippy and bright."[8] However, a critic for the *Bulletin of the Center for Children's Books*, a publication for teachers, was not so impressed: "This humorous, episodic, but weakly constructed story [is] told by Jason in a lively style that is marred by a plethora of flippancy."[9] (In other words, it was too jokey.)

However, Spinelli would remain fond of *Space Station Seventh Grade*. As late as 2002, he told a fan that it was his favorite book. He's said that of all of his characters in all of his novels, he has the most in common with Jason.

Wartime

Jason may have been the most similar to Spinelli, but the character whom he liked the most was the female star of his next book. *Who Put That Hair in My Toothbrush?* "was inspired by two of our kids, Molly and Jeffrey," Spinelli said. "They were always fighting, so I decided to write a story about sibling warfare. I figured if they wouldn't be friends in real life, I could make them so by the end of my book."[10]

Toothbrush is told by fourteen-year-old Greg Tofer (a neat, tidy boy, like Jerry) and his twelve-year-old sister, Megin, in alternating chapters: one in Greg's voice, the next in Megin's. *Like Space Station Seventh Grade*, it's a bunch of episodes such as Megin's destroying Greg's science project and Greg's tossing Megin's hockey stick into an icy pond.

Spinelli said in 1997 that *Toothbrush* may have been his toughest book to write: "It was hard to figure out how to keep the story moving when it was being told from two different point of views."[11]

Still, he managed to finish the book, which appeared in print two years after *Space Station Seventh Grade*. A reviewer for the *Washington Post* newspaper called Spinelli "a master of those embarrassing, gloppy, painful, and suddenly wonderful things that happen on the razor's edge between childhood and full-fledged adolescence."[12] A commentator in *English Journal,* a teachers' magazine, praised passages of the book as "unbelievably funny."[13]

Well after its first reviews, *Toothbrush* would continue impressing readers. Four years after its publication, it was nominated for the 1988 Indian Paintbrush Book Award, which children in Wyoming give to their favorite book. And the *Los Angeles Times* reported in 1996 that the hockey-loving Megin inspired a fifteen-year-old girl named Ev Hee Han to join a mostly male hockey team.

A Teenage Mouse

The year after *Toothbrush*, Spinelli switched from writing for young teenagers to writing for an older group. In 1985's *Night of the Whale*, would-be writer Mouse Umlau shares a beachside vacation house with a few friends the week after they graduate from Avon Oaks High School. As Spinelli was, Mouse is an obedient boy, but he isn't sure how obedient he should be.

> It was Sunday. Should I go to church? For the first time in my life I had to answer that question; it wouldn't be decided for me . . .
>
> Looking at it from the longest-range view I could manage—far beyond my mother saying as I walked out the door, "Don't forget church on Sunday"—I had no doubt that I *Ought* to go . . .
>
> The answer came sharp and clear, crystallized courtesy of my mother: I probably would have gone on my own, but you messed up my freedom of choice by telling me to. So the answer is no. You blew it, Mom.[14]

Night tells how the inexperienced Mouse reacts to his first time getting drunk, spending time alone, being far from home with a gorgeous girl, and having other adventures. Finally—in exploits that fill the last third of the book—he and his friends try to rescue beached whales.

Night earned some of the most critical comments of Spinelli's career. A *School Library Journal* reviewer attacked the book's "crude and crudely described activities," found fault with its "seemingly interminable [endless] string of descriptions of beer guzzling," and predicted, "Many teens won't stay around until day five of this hedonistic week . . . Those who do will have a hard time buying it."[15] This type of reaction gave Spinelli "a sort of reputation as a bad-boy of juvenile letters,"[16] said *School Library Journal* writer Robert Unsworth.

Spinelli has never said whether the reaction to *Night* bothered him, but he has never again written a book about characters as old as Mouse.

Back to Jason

In 1986, Spinelli returned to the world of *Space Station Seventh Grade* with the book *Jason and Marceline*. The work begins about a year after *Space Station* ends, with the characters entering ninth grade. Like the young Jerry Spinelli, Jason wonders if he's got what it takes to be truly masculine. To find out, he does to one of his schoolmates what Spinelli did to Joey Stackhouse:

> How did I ever expect to win respect? Get a girl? *Keep* a girl?
> I had to hit somebody . . .
> After school, I caught up to [Little Looie Lopezia] a couple of blocks away. He was

lugging his suitcase-radio, blasting the neighborhood . . .

I hit him . . .

That's when he started to cry. His face fell apart, his eyes flooded, he hugged his radio to his chest. "You b-basterd!" he blubbered, and he ran off . . .

I didn't feel so good. Why did he have to start bawling like that? Why couldn't he be a man about it? Was he trying to spoil the whole thing?[17]

Even more important to Jason is the quirky, painfully direct, not conventionally feminine Marceline McAllister. Jason can't figure out if they are steady dates, just friends, or something else. Meanwhile, his hormones are bursting, and he wants much more from Marceline (and other girls) than the few quick kisses that he gets.

"Spinelli captures perfectly the adolescent boy who supposedly has a sexual thought every seven seconds," *Los Angeles Times* reviewer Gloria Miklowitz wrote. "[I]t's a book kids of either sex—from sixth grade through ninth—will love."[18] "Spinelli's teenagers are fresh and funny, sometimes crude, sometimes poignant [touching], and always very real,"[19] said a writer for *Publishers Weekly*. A *School Library Journal* critic pointed out, "It's all done for laughs, and

Spinelli can be very funny, if very crude. Some adults will shudder or sputter over this one, but YAs [young adults] will love it."[20] Although such reviews prompt one to think that the book is filled with sex, it actually contains few scenes of physical contact.

Going Younger

In *Dump Days* (1988), Spinelli's next book, eleven-year-old friends Duke Pickwell and J. D. Kidd are out of school for the summer when they decide to make one day absolutely perfect. Their plans include buying their favorite foods, pedaling bikes just ahead of an oncoming truck, playing the town's best arcade game, and more. Since most of these activities cost money, they try various schemes to get it.

A reviewer in *Publishers Weekly* stated, "Spinelli spins a story that weaves together the shared conversations and small-town adventures of a friendship based on trust, humor, compassion and imagination."[21] A reviewer for the *Bulletin of the Center for Children's Books*, another important magazine for kids' books, praised "Spinelli's convincing portrait of a solid friendship and the freshly comic character-izations of the supporting cast."[22]

Meanwhile, Spinelli was making a huge decision. In 1989, after more than two decades at Chilton, he quit his job to write full-time. It was a risky move. Many writers of children's books don't sell enough to support a house full of kids. The Spinellis didn't have much money, and they had less and less after Spinelli stopped getting Chilton's regular paychecks. However, he kept writing, and 1990 saw the publication of *The Bathwater Gang*, starring J. D. Kidd's spunky little sister, Bertie. In the book, Bertie is bored one summer until her energetic grandmother encourages her to start a kid gang. Unfortunately, Bertie can get only one person to join—Duke Pickwell's sister, Damaris—and faces opposition from a gang of boys. A reviewer in *School Library Journal* called *Bathwater* "light [and] entertaining."[23]

Up until this point, Spinelli's novels told stories about more or less realistic kids, but his next book was a tall tale about a legendary hero. It drew on Spinelli's childhood more than any book since *Space Station Seventh Grade*. And it made him famous.

Its name was *Maniac Magee*.

5 Fame from a Maniac

A runaway in every sense of the word, eleven-year-old orphan Jeffrey "Maniac" Magee spends much of his book sprinting through Two Mills, a fictional town in Pennsylvania. Along the way, he hits baseballs off a pitcher who strikes everyone else out, faces up to bullies who scare whole neighborhoods, unravels a massive knot that no one else can untie, and finally unites the town's very separate blacks and whites. He's so important that he was actually mentioned well before his book was published. The first appearance of his name came in *Dump Days*: "Maniac Magee [is] an orphan sort of kid, who sleeps at the bandshell."[1] That Spinelli mentioned Maniac in *Dump Days,* about two years before *Maniac Magee,* shows how long he had been thinking about the character.

He began *Maniac* the way he had started other books. As he says, "It was simply time to write my next book, so I paged through my notes, and the idea that caught my attention most was a story about a kid who is a hero to other kids. That was the launchpad idea. Everything followed from that: a patchwork of memory, invention, [and] observation."[2]

Spinelli had tried at least twice before to tell Maniac's story but couldn't get its mythic yet believable tone right. (As he says early on in *Maniac,* "Be very, very careful not to let the facts get mixed up with the truth."[3]) "[Spinelli] was frustrated and decided to take a vacation from the book," journalist Jennifer Brown wrote. "No sooner had he turned his back on it than the opening line popped into his head. 'I was in my office [at home] one night doing something else, and that's when the words came to me: "They say Maniac Magee was born in a dump,"' [Spinelli] recalls. 'I've never had the sense that I reached down and took hold of that sentence. It simply came to me.'"[4] Still, the book took more than a year to write, longer than most of Spinelli's other books.

Maniac uses the places and people of Spinelli's youth. Maniac's love for an old man is like the author's love for his own grandfather. Spinelli's knowledge of sports helps bring Maniac's athletic victories to life. Even his regret that he didn't read or write much as a boy surfaced in Maniac. "That's why I have Maniac Magee carrying a book in his hand as he's running along the tracks or going to play baseball," Spinelli explains. "It's as though I'm kicking it the second time around, and this time, doggone it, I'm going to do it right."[5]

Then there's race. Maniac's greatest miracle is bringing blacks and whites together. It comes about because Maniac, like young Spinelli, just can't see differences between races or understand why they dislike each other.

Spinelli liked *Maniac Magee*. In 2000 he was asked, "If you could recommend only one of your novels for us to read, which one would it be?" His answer: *"Maniac Magee*—for the message, the story, and the language."[6] But in 1990, when the book was published, he wasn't sure how the world would react. "I had doubts that any book called *Maniac Magee* would be taken seriously by award committees,"[7] he said.

However, critics loved the book. A review in *Publishers Weekly* called it "a humorous yet poignant look at the issue of race relations," and added, "[t]his off-the-wall yarn will give readers of all colors plenty of food for thought."[8] Even the famous *New York Times Book Review* offered praise, observing that *Maniac* "has the tone of a story that has come down through the years."[9] By the end of 1990, *Maniac Magee* had received an award for outstanding fiction, given annually by *The Horn Book Magazine* (a children's literature magazine) and the *Boston Globe* newspaper.

All this acclaim didn't bring much money, though. Spinelli confessed that by the start of 1991, he was ready for a full-time office job.

Newbery News

On January 13, 1991, Spinelli would later recall:

> I was doing what all respectable Penn-sylvanians were doing at 12:30 AM, a half-hour after midnight: I was sleeping . . . [The telephone rang.] "Hello?" I say.
>
> The voice that responds is unfamiliar to me. A doctor? The voice tells me its name is Alice Naylor [of the American Library Association]. It says something like, "We want you to know that we have been very careful not to let the facts get mixed up with the truth." It says the word *Newbery*.
>
> The rest is fuzzy.[10]

Spinelli had won the John Newbery Medal, awarded by the American Library Association each year to honor the year's best book for children. The Newbery virtually guarantees that libraries and bookstores will recommend the book.

"Among Jerry's first words during the 12:30 AM phone call to announce the news of his award: 'Is this a joke?'"[11] said Newbery judge Mary Blandin Bauer. By now, the call had awakened Eileen. As Spinelli remembered, "We talk, pace, giggle, drink Poland Spring [bottled] water. At 4 AM we go back to bed. We sleep straight through to 4:15. At 7 AM, we give up, go out to the Vale-Rio diner, have breakfast. I order French toast. I never get bacon. I get bacon. We come back home. We sleep till noon.

"And now again the phone starts ringing. This time, there is no stopping it."[12] The calls come from journalists who want to interview Spinelli about his book and his medal. By the morning of January 15, the news is all over.

Maniac Magee outsold all of Spinelli's other books. In June, he traveled to Atlanta, Georgia, to receive his Newbery Medal. In October, he gave the opening speech at the St. Louis Public Library Children's Literature Festival. Schoolkids in Wisconsin voted *Maniac* the Golden Archer

Award for their favorite book, and the Pennsylvania Library Association's Youth Services Division gave *Maniac* its Carolyn W. Field Award as the year's best novel.

The Wonder Year

Spinelli wasn't just accepting awards in 1991. He also published more books that year than in any other to date. As Spinelli later recalled, "I read a [newspaper] story about a girl who competed on her high-school wrestling team. A year later, bookstores carried a new book with my name on it: *There's a Girl in My Hammerlock*."[13]

Hammerlock is eighth-grader Maisie Potter's response to a newspaper article about the first girl on her school's all-boy wrestling team: Maisie herself. Nearly nobody wants her on the squad, and Maisie has to fight for respect.

She got it from the critics. A reviewer in *Publishers Weekly* wrote, "Maisie is an eminently [extremely] likable character, and her trials and triumphs make for a highly satisfying tale."[14] A review in *School Library Journal* agreed: "Maisie is strong yet vulnerable, and young teens will relate to her . . . This would be useful in libraries for units on sports, friendship, family, peer pressure, strong female characters—and just for pleasure."[15]

As late as 1994, three years after it was published, *Hammerlock* received the state of New York's Charlotte Award for best young adult fiction.

Also in 1991 came *Fourth Grade Rats*, which takes its title from a schoolyard rhyme that starts the book:

> First grade babies!
> Second grade cats!
> Third grade angels!
> Fourth grade . . . RRRRRATS![16]

The lead character, new fourth-grader Suds Morton, doesn't want to be a rat—that is, a kid who is tough, hard, and manly enough to defy his mother, push smaller kids off swings, and never, ever cry. It's not easy because he's just not very tough. For instance, he's been in love since age six with a girl named Judy Billings—much like Spinelli, who by age seven had a girlfriend named Judy Brooks. But when his best friend pressures Suds into rat-ness, Suds has to decide—like Jason in *Jason and Marceline* and Mouse in *Night of the Whale*—what being a real man is all about.

"Rapid-fire dialogue and a hilarious string of episodes," said a reviewer in *Publishers Weekly*, "unfold a story with a valuable message about peer pressure and the importance of being oneself."[17] "The humor here is broad but genuinely comical, while the kids' real concerns are presented with sympathy,"[18] stated a critic in *Kirkus Reviews*.

Spinelli's other 1991 book was the first of a series. *Report to the Principal's Office* is about four sixth-grade kids adjusting to life in a new school led by a cheerful, quirky principal. Of the kids—quiet and sometimes wimpy Eddie Mott, sharp-eyed writer Salem Brownmiller, grumpy beauty Sunny Wyler, and crafty, inventive Pickles Johnson—Eddie is nearly a stand-in for a younger Spinelli. He's a tidy, obedient boy who, like Spinelli, gets assigned the job of raising the school's flag.

In 1992's *Who Ran My Underwear Up the Flagpole?*, Eddie is on the school's football team, which Salem manages; Sunny has taken up cheerleading; and Pickles is in the marching band. In *Do the Funky Pickle*, also from 1992, Pickles and Salem try to teach Eddie how to dance so he can impress Sunny. And in 1993's *Picklemania*, the characters get tied up in mysterious romantic entanglements.

Though these books didn't get the kind of attention that *Maniac Magee* did, a *School Library Journal* reviewer called Spinelli's *Report to the Principal's Office* "a book written with sparkle, humor, and warmth."[19]

Back to *Bathwater*

"Snappy dialogue; a good moral or two; and simple, fun reading."[20] Those are the words of a review in *The Horn Book Magazine* describing Spinelli's next book, *The Bathwater Gang Gets Down to Business* (1992). This reappearance of Bertie Kidd finds her, like her big brother, J. D., in *Dump Days*, inventing ways to make money to pay for a great time—in Bertie's case, a trip to the circus. "This sunny, lightweight chapter book," said a reviewer in *Booklist*, "is perfect for the age group [that will read it]."[21]

Meanwhile, throughout 1992 and 1993, *Maniac Magee* received more favorable attention. In eighteen states and two Canadian provinces, kids voted it their favorite book. In June 1992, white fifth-graders and black sixth-graders in Massachusetts put on a stage production of the story. And in August 1993, agents for twelve-year-old actor and *Maniac Magee* fan Elijah Wood (later star of *Lord of the Rings*) bought the rights to make the book into a movie. Wood planned to play *Maniac* but never did, which is not unusual in Hollywood.

Filmmakers often buy the rights to books without turning them into movies.

Maniac wasn't the only Spinelli book getting recognition. In 1994, students in Wyoming nominated *There's a Girl in My Hammerlock* for the Indian Paintbrush Award, while California students gave the book the Young Reader Medal, for the one book per year that they like best.

However, in Evergreen, Colorado, close to where Spinelli had been stationed during part of his military service, Wilmot Elementary School principal Larry Fayer ordered school librarian Thresa Marsh to remove *There's a Girl in My Hammerlock, Who Put That Hair in My Toothbrush?*, and forty other books from the shelves. Some parents thought that the books contained "gratuitous [needless] violence and foul language,"[22] according to the *Rocky Mountain News*.

That complaint was just a small bump in the otherwise smooth road that Spinelli's books were traveling. In 1995 students in South Carolina and Maryland voted *Fourth Grade Rats* their favorite novel.

Amid all this activity, Spinelli didn't stop writing, although he did slow down. While he had two books published in 1990, three in 1991, and three in 1992, only one (*Picklemania*) came out in 1993 and none in 1994. In 1995, though, Spinelli was back with *Tooter Pepperday*.

Tooter Tales

After nine-year-old Tooter's dad quits his job to write books, much as Spinelli himself had done in 1989, Tooter's family needs to save money. They move from Tooter's beloved small-city home to her aunt's farm, where they can live for free. However, Tooter misses her old home, as Spinelli did when his family moved during his high school days.

Tooter tries to sabotage the move. One of her attacks was inspired by the Spinellis' daughter Molly. Spinelli's publisher recalled the incident: "While writing one of his books, Jerry didn't hear his daughter calling him until she sat on his desk and began writing him a note vertically along the page of his longhand manuscript."[23] The incident found its way into *Tooter Pepperday*:

> Tooter found her father at his computer . . .
>   She coughed to get his attention. He kept pecking. When Mr. Pepperday was writing, he forgot the rest of the world.
>   She sat on the keyboard.
>   He noticed.

The screen went crazy. Mr. Pepperday went crazy. His nose glowed red like a Christmas-tree bulb.

He bellowed: "TOOTERRRRRR! Scoot!"

Tooter scooted . . .

Next day Mr. Pepperday sat down to his computer. He punched up the chapter book he was working on. Here is what appeared on the screen:

Tooter Pepperday was a wonderful girl. She was kind and friendly and nice to everybody. She lived in Morgantown. She loved her home. She loved to play with her friends. And then her mean and cruel parents took her away to a smelly old farm.[24]

"There are enough farm jokes and silly scenes," said a writer in *Booklist*, "to keep readers turning the pages."[25] A reviewer in *The Horn Book Magazine* called it "a good, sound story,"[26] and a commentator for *The Bulletin of the Center for Children's Books* said, "The broad humor and mischievous heroine will appeal to new readers both urban and rural."[27]

Crash and Penn

Spinelli's next book, *Crash* (1996), would be more serious. In *Crash*, seventh-grader Crash Coogan, a football star and local bully, is confused and frustrated by his oddball neighbor, Penn Webb. Penn is a nonviolent boy, a vegetarian rather than a meat-eater like Crash, and a cheerleader rather than an athlete. Crash looks for ways to give Penn a hard time, but just as Maniac Magee doesn't understand racism, the good-natured Penn doesn't understand Crash's contempt.

Spinelli has said that the Penn Relays, a local race that forms the book's climax, inspired *Crash* and gave Penn Webb his name. Spinelli's own childhood experiences with athletics probably helped, too. In any event, *School Library Journal* and the American Library Association listed *Crash* among the year's best books. In Nevada, Wyoming, Minnesota, and Massachusetts, kids voted *Crash* their favorite book of the year. Even years later, in 2000, the book won awards in Wisconsin and North Carolina.

Some readers did have criticisms. *Booklist*, for instance, complained, "The plot becomes rather predictable,"[28] but praised the book's characters and humor. *The Horn Book Magazine* noted, "Spinelli deals with intriguing themes in a fast-paced, readable novel," but it found Penn "too good to be true."[29] Nevertheless, *Crash* earned Spinelli more awards and honors than any book except *Maniac Magee*.

Four in One

After *Crash*, Spinelli switched gears. All of his stories up to that point had been book-length tales. But 1997's *The Library Card*—a book suggested by Spinelli's editor, Ann Reit—was a collection of four stories, connected only by a single object: a library card that changes the lives of the kids who acquire it.

In "Mongoose," the card entices twelve-year-old vandal Jamie "Mongoose" Hill away from spray-painting graffiti. "Brenda" finds TV lover Brenda Foster suffering through a week without television until the card gives her something else to hold her attention. (Spinelli understood TV addiction from his own childhood. In third grade, when a kidney disease kept him in bed, he complained so much that his parents finally let him go downstairs to watch TV.) In "April Mendez," the card helps the title character form a bond with a knife-wielding runaway. "Sonseray" shows the card's power to help the most desperate kid in any Spinelli book, a homeless orphan who twists his painful need for mothering into acts of cruelty. "Of the four stories, I feel particularly attached to 'Sonseray,' though his kidhood does not resemble my own at all,"[30] Spinelli said.

The book received a good, if not spectacular, response. "Spinelli is a shrewd storyteller, balancing lighter moments with provocative ones to meaningful effect,"[31] said a writer for *Kirkus Reviews*. A reviewer for the teachers' magazine *Childhood Education* praised the stories as "funny, sad, and thought-provoking."[32] And the American Library Association voted *The Library Card* one of 1997's best books for young adults.

Wringing It Out

Spinelli's next book idea came to him, like *There's a Girl in My Hammerlock*, when he read a newspaper article—this time about a pigeon shoot. The article inspired him so much that he created his own article. It became the first page of *Wringer*:

> WAYMER—Hundreds of sharpshooters in and around this rural community are cleaning their shotguns as they look forward to Saturday's 63rd annual Pigeon Day. Beginning at around 8 AM, participants who have paid a

fee will each have the chance to shoot at ten to twenty pigeons as they are released from boxes . . .

All downed birds are retrieved by so-called wringer boys, who break the necks of the wounded and place all bodies in plastic bags.[33]

In Waymer, being a wringer proves that a boy is becoming a real man. Nine-year-old Palmer LaRue is closing in on the age when he, like every other boy in town, will become a wringer. But Palmer feels the way that Jerry did as a teenager, when the terror of being drafted made him fear his birthdays.

He did not want to be a wringer.

This was one of the first things he had learned about himself . . . [but] he could not escape it any more than he could escape himself . . .

He would come to it as surely as nine follows eight and ten follows nine . . . He would get there simply by growing one day older.[34]

"Stunning"[35] and "spellbinding"[36] were some of the words that critics used to describe *Wringer*. Reviewers from publications ranging from the scholarly *Journal of Adolescent & Adult Literacy* to the popular *New York Times Book Review* praised it. Even publications that found faults in the story liked it. A *Booklist* critic, for instance, called one of the book's main characters unconvincing but added, "the combination of a tender, sometimes comic pet story with the bloody public festival will move kids."[37]

Wringer soon began piling up awards. *School Library Journal* and *Booklist* named it one of 1997's best books. In January 1998, the Newbery committee named *Wringer* an "honor book"—that is, a runner-up for the Newbery Medal. The Pennsylvania Library Association gave the novel the Carolyn W. Field Award, making Spinelli the only author to win it twice.

In January 1999, Spinelli traveled to Georgia to receive the Milner Award, which Atlanta area students give annually to their favorite author. The next year, students in Maryland and Wyoming voted *Wringer* onto lists of their favorite books.

The Return of Tooter

Nearly ignored amid all this praise was Spinelli's *Blue Ribbon Blues*, a sequel to *Tooter Pepperday*. In the new book, published in 1998, Tooter still doesn't like farm life, but she's determined to show other farm people that she's as good as them. She decides to enter a goat in a competition at the county fair, but nothing goes as she expects.

Blue Ribbon Blues received some nice responses from critics. A reviewer in *School Library Journal,* for instance, called the book "light, fast-paced and humorous . . . a pleasant addition to the paperback rack."[38] Nevertheless, the book didn't generate nearly as much attention or excitement as *Wringer*. It didn't sell terribly well, either. The book seemed easy to overlook, sandwiched between the wrenching *Wringer* and Spinelli's next project. That book was nothing like he'd ever written before. But in a sense, too, it was like everything that he'd written.

6 *Knots* and Beyond

Jerry Spinelli has hinted that a kid inspired him to write *Knots in My Yo-yo String*—subtitled the *Autobiography of a Kid*. He was visiting North Dakota to pick up an award for *Maniac Magee* when a boy in the audience asked, "Do you think being a kid helped you to become a writer?" Spinelli's answer: "Yes, I believe it has."[1] *Knots* explains that answer. It describes some of the events, places, and people in real life that have seeped into Spinelli's books.

Knots received good reviews. A *Children's Literature* magazine critic noted, "It is a great way for students to learn how an author uses his experiences."[2] A reviewer for the teachers' magazine *Instructor* called it "honest and moving."[3] And a writer in *The Horn Book Magazine* praised "the author's keen powers of observation."[4]

With *Knots* in 1998, Spinelli had seen fifteen of his books published in eight years. That's not an easy pace to maintain. His next book wouldn't appear for another two years. In fact, he'd been working on it, on and off, since 1966.

Carried Away by Caraway

"At first, it was going to be about a boy," Spinelli said of *Stargirl* (his next book). "Many things I read over the years influenced the story, notably the play *Ondine*."[5] In the play—about an impulsive teenager—a man who loves her says, "She would bring [me] all the delight and tenderness and goodness [I] would ever know . . . [But] she says whatever comes into her head—and the things that come into that girl's head!"[6]

Strange things come into teenage Stargirl Caraway's head, too, and she's not shy about letting them out. She sings at her classmates, laughs and dances when no one else is laughing or dancing, and cheers for the basketball team that her school is trying to beat. At first, schoolmate

Leo Borlock can't figure her out. Eventually, though, he falls in love with her, but Stargirl's weird ways drive virtually every other student to resent and shun her. When they turn on Leo as well, he has to make some difficult choices.

Said a critic in the *Christian Science Monitor*, "Spinelli gives us stellar [outstanding] writing and a wondrous, slightly magical heroine."[7] "Poetic,"[8] said a *New York Times* reviewer. The American Library Association listed *Stargirl* on its roster of the year's best novels for young adults.

Not everyone was so thrilled. "[Stargirl's] naïvete is overplayed and annoying," said a *Booklist* critic.[9] A reviewer in *The Horn Book Magazine* noted that *Stargirl* had "much heavy-handed moralizing."[10] The book's ending disappointed a writer for *School Library Journal*, who added, "The prose lapses into occasionally unfortunate flowery flights."[11]

While *Stargirl* was attracting comments, Spinelli himself earned some honors. In Oklahoma, the Tulsa City-County Library gave him its Anne V. Zarrow Award, presented "to nationally acclaimed authors who have made a significant contribution to the field of literature for children and young adults."[12] In June, he gave a talk to dignitaries in Philadelphia to help the local school district and other advocates of reading kick off a summer reading drive; the district gave every sixth grader a copy of *Maniac Magee*. And the International Reading Association, a group of more than three hundred thousand teachers, librarians, and others in ninety-nine countries, profiled Spinelli in *The Newbery Award*, a video about the medal.

September 2001 found Spinelli doing a book signing at Gettysburg College. And in November, he and Eileen (by now a published author herself) gave a reading and talk at Swarthmore College, near Philadelphia. Spinelli read the first chapter of his next book, *Loser*.

Winning with *Loser*

"Donald Zinkoff," said a writer for *Kirkus Reviews*, "can't sit still, can't stop laughing, falls over his own feet, adores school and silly words and his family, is prone to throwing up due to a defective stomach valve, is impervious to peer pressure, and never frets about being perennially [constantly] last in any competition."[13] As a result, people find Zinkoff as confusing and annoying as Stargirl Caraway, Penn Webb, or Maniac Magee.

But the best model for Zinkoff may be Louis Darden, a childhood friend of Spinelli's. As

Spinelli wrote in his autobiography, Louis didn't worry about always being last in sports and, like Zinkoff, laughed at inappropriate times. His attitude angered the young Spinelli.

As an adult, though, Spinelli felt differently. He said after *Loser* was published, "I admire people with the courage to be themselves. I admire people who value other people. I admire people who don't give up. Zinkoff is all of these."[14] And Spinelli certainly wasn't alone in his admiration of Zinkoff. A *Booklist* reviewer observed, "It's impossible to dislike sunny, sweet-spirited Donald,"[15] but also noted that it's hard to believe that Zinkoff doesn't notice how much his schoolmates dislike him. A *Reading Today* magazine writer stated that *Loser* is "told with wit and warmth."[16] And *The Horn Book Magazine* called it "a wonderful character study."[17]

On Beyond *Loser*

At the time of this writing, it is too soon to know if *Loser*, published in 2002, will win as much acclaim and popularity as *Maniac Magee*. However, it's certain that it won't be ignored. Spinelli's name on a book jacket always attracts readers. His books have appeared in Brazil, England, Italy, Japan, and Korea. The cable TV channel Nickelodeon has

made a *Maniac Magee* movie, and various production companies have bought the rights to turn
Stargirl, Crash, and *Wringer* into movies.

Meanwhile, Spinelli has continued to write.
In 2003, he published a picture book, *My Daddy
and Me.* The next book will be a novel; he hasn't
said much about it except that "it will take place
during the Holocaust."[18] He's also talked about
writing a science-fiction novel.

But writing such books isn't easy. Spinelli's
method of creating stories involves hard work,
deep thought, and about two hundred fifty
ballpoint pens.

7 How He Does It

As Spinelli recalled in 1991, "Not long ago, a kid in a group I was speaking to raised his hand and said, 'Where do you get all that stuff [in your books]?'" Spinelli responded by saying, "'You. You're where I get all that stuff . . . I get it from the me that used to be you. From my own kids, your age-mates."[1]

As Spinelli says, "You keep your eyes and ears open."[2]

Getting Ideas

Spinelli works by listening and observing—and whatever he hears and sees, he writes down. As he says, "If you went around and counted, you'd probably find 250 ballpoint pens in my house, so I just make notes whenever things occur to me."[3]

Deciding which notes to turn into books can be tough. It's not easy for Spinelli to decide on the one that will make a good book. But he's developed a rule that guides him. "Write what you care about," he says. "If you care about your topic, you'll do your best writing, and then you stand the best chance of really touching a reader in some way."[4]

More specifically, he's said: "One of the first things you do as an author is figure what would kids at [a particular] age be dealing with and interested in, and then you just rummage back through your memory and your observations and come up with things that seem to matter."[5]

From Ideas to Books

After Spinelli assembles ideas that matter, he writes down any thoughts that the ideas bring to mind. From there, he writes a first draft. Along the way, he constantly refines and fixes his writing to make sure that his readers can believe that his characters would actually say and do what he writes.

Many other writers create draft after draft, rewriting the book over and over. Not Spinelli. As he says, "I guess I didn't learn to write that way because I didn't have the time. I was writing on my lunch hour, on weekends, and after dinner, so I just didn't have time to do all that."[6]

Besides, writing isn't easy. As Spinelli says, "[There's] seldom a day when I feel like writing . . . but it's part of the territory. Writing doesn't do itself. One way or another, I get down to it and get something done."[7] An online interviewer asked him, "If there was a hidden camera recording everything you did as you wrote your books, what would it show us?" Spinelli answered: "It would show me sitting in front of this computer with a blank look on my face, wondering what the heck to write next."[8]

A Way of Life

For years, Spinelli has written in an office inside his home. He says, "My office is spacious, plenty of room for my desk near the door, my computer/writing console in one corner, filing cabinet in another corner."[9] On the walls are, among other things, a painting that became the cover of *Space Station Seventh Grade*, plus several of Spinelli's awards. "I even wrote away for a gizmo that makes ocean sounds to cover background noise, but there's no surf that's a match for six kids."[10]

Whether kids are present or not, "morning is my main writing time, basically from 10 till noon . . . As I prepare to write in the morning, I close my office door, and I read several pages of a book that I find meaningful . . . Then I read a page from a kind of writer's 'daily devotional' called *Walking on Alligators*."[11] The book includes observations like "The only way to write is to write today" and "Writing can feel like stepping off into thin air. Some of us can write no other way."[12]

When Spinelli finishes a manuscript, he shows it to his wife, Eileen. And if she dislikes something, he generally changes it. From there, the book goes to his publisher and eventually out into the world. No doubt it'll find an appreciative audience.

Even if it doesn't, Spinelli will always be a writer. "This is the way I explain it to kids . . . If you're coming to school on the bus this morning, and as you're zooming by Tenth Street, you see on the corner one of the most incredible things you've ever seen, what are you going to do as soon as you get to school?

"Everybody's hand goes up. They know the answer. 'I'm going to tell my friends.'

"That's it. There's a natural urge in everyone to communicate."[13]

Fortunately for his readers, Jerry Spinelli has obeyed that urge for more than twenty years—and plans to keep obeying it for many more.

Interview with Jerry Spinelli

DAVID SEIDMAN: In your autobiography, you mention your paternal grandfather and the impact that he made on you. What effect, if any, did your other grandparents have?

JERRY SPINELLI: My maternal grandmother died before I was born. My maternal grandfather died when I was very young. My only memory of him is bringing me a banana whenever he came to visit.

DAVID SEIDMAN: Do you name characters or base their personality traits after people you know?

JERRY SPINELLI: Personality traits, yes; whole characters, no. There are snippets of people I've known throughout my cast of characters. A good example is Megin (Megamouth) from *Who Put That Hair in My Toothbrush?* Megin is feisty, sloppy, and loyal—traits shared with the girl who inspired the character, our daughter Molly. But in other ways, Megin differs from Molly.

DAVID SEIDMAN: You've mostly written novels about kids. Do you want to write other kinds of books, like novels about adults, nonfiction for kids or adults?

JERRY SPINELLI: I used to think about writing adult books, and then I realized, hey, I already *am* writing for adults. When I sit down to write, I don't think to myself, I'm writing for kids. As far as I'm concerned, I'm writing for everybody. Take books like *Maniac Magee* or *Stargirl*. If I were asked to edit those books for an adult edition, I wouldn't change a thing.

DAVID SEIDMAN: What do your wife, children, and grandchildren think about the books that you write? Do they have any favorites among your books?

JERRY SPINELLI: My wife and fellow author, Eileen, reads and evaluates each chapter as it comes off the printer. I think the kids (six) appreciate my authorship more now than they did when they were in school. And the grandkids (sixteen) like to tell teachers and librarians who their grandfather is.

DAVID SEIDMAN: Do your children and grandchildren expect you to eavesdrop on them so that you can learn how they act and speak, and work that knowledge into your books?

JERRY SPINELLI: Not that I know of. Molly notwithstanding, I've made minimal use of my kids and grandkids as source material. I'm always taking in material from everyday life. And I get a lot from memories of my own kidhood.

DAVID SEIDMAN: Sometimes, you bring characters from one novel back in sequels. *Space Station Seventh Grade*'s Jason Herkimer, for example, came back in *Jason and Marceline*; you've written two books about Tooter Pepperday; and the Principal's Posse from *Report to the Principal's Office* showed up in three sequels. What makes you bring some characters back while leaving other characters in just one book?

JERRY SPINELLI: *Report to the Principal's Office* was the first in a four-book series I agreed to write, so repeating characters was a given from the start. The second Tooter Pepperday book, *Blue Ribbon Blues*, was the publisher's suggestion, too, as I recall. Generally, I don't like to write or read sequels. They're seldom as good as the originals.

DAVID SEIDMAN: Can you predict if a book is going to be popular and sell well? How does it feel when a book sells very well—and when it doesn't sell well at all?

JERRY SPINELLI: No. If I could predict, every publisher in the world would have me on retainer. As for selling well, I write in part to make a connection, to touch a reader. When that happens, I'm happy.

DAVID SEIDMAN: You've said that you bounce from idea to idea. How do you know when you have an idea good enough for you to stick with it and turn it into a novel?

JERRY SPINELLI: Great ideas are a special, rare thing. But good ideas, frankly, are a dime a dozen. Often the critical factor is not in recognizing a good idea when you see one but in executing it into a good story.

DAVID SEIDMAN: What's the hardest part of writing a book? What's the easiest part? Has writing a book gotten easier or harder as you've written more and more?

JERRY SPINELLI: The easiest part is starting out. First pages, like good ideas, are a dime a dozen. In my opinion the hardest part of writing a book—sometimes—is getting onto the page and into the reader the same picture and feeling that I have inside me.

DAVID SEIDMAN: What writers do you read and admire—especially children's book writers? What have you learned from them? Have any of them been a great influence on you in terms of subject matter or style?

JERRY SPINELLI: Frankly, other than Eileen Spinelli, I don't read children's book writers regularly. I feel I need to get away from my own game each day. When I think of influences on my own writing, I think back to the one author I read every day when I was a kid—Red McCarthy, sports editor of my hometown newspaper.

DAVID SEIDMAN: Writing a book can mean lots of rewriting. How do you know when you're done?

JERRY SPINELLI: When I can't think of any way to make it better, or when I'm sick of it, whichever comes first. I don't write multiple drafts. I don't do a whole lot of rewriting. I see writing as a kind of performance art, an activity, almost a sport. The writer I am today is different from the writer I will be tomorrow.

Timeline

1886 Jerry Spinelli's grandfather Alessandro "Alex" Spinelli is born in Italy.

1900 Alex Spinelli travels to America.

1909 Alex and his wife, Millie, have a son, Louis.

1933 Louis Spinelli meets Lorna Bigler.

May 16, 1936 Louis Spinelli marries Lorna Bigler.

February 1, 1941 Lorna gives birth to a son, Jerry.

July 29, 1945 Lorna gives birth to Jerry's brother, Bill.

October 1957 Spinelli writes "Goal to Go," the poem that starts him on the road to becoming a writer.

1963 Spinelli graduates from Gettysburg College.

1964 Spinelli completes the Writing Seminars at Johns Hopkins University.

1965 Spinelli joins the United States Naval Air Reserve.

1966 Spinelli starts work at the Chilton Company, editing magazines. In his spare time, he writes novels. He starts making notes that will become the novel *Stargirl*.

Mid-1960s Spinelli meets Eileen Mesi, a secretary at Chilton.

1969 Jerry Spinelli completes his first novel. It is rejected by every publisher who sees it.

May 21, 1977 Spinelli marries Eileen Mesi.

1981 Spinelli completes *Space Station Seventh Grade*, his first novel about teenagers.

1982 Little, Brown and Company publishes *Space Station Seventh Grade*.

1984 Little, Brown publishes *Who Put That Hair in My Toothbrush?*

1985 Little, Brown publishes *Night of the Whale*.

1986 Little, Brown publishes *Jason and Marceline*, the sequel to *Space Station Seventh Grade*.

1988 Little, Brown publishes *Dump Days*, the first book to mention Maniac Magee.

1989 Spinelli quits his job at Chilton to write full-time.

1990 Little, Brown publishes *The Bathwater Gang*, featuring characters from *Dump Days*. Little, Brown publishes *Maniac Magee*.

1991 *Maniac Magee* wins the Newbery Medal. Scholastic Inc. publishes *Fourth Grade Rats*. Simon & Schuster publishes *There's a Girl in My Hammerlock* and *Report to the Principal's Office*.

1992 Little, Brown publishes *The Bathwater Gang Gets Down to Business*, the sequel to *The Bathwater Gang*. Scholastic publishes *Who Ran My Underwear Up the Flagpole?* and *Do the Funky Pickle*, sequels to *Report to the Principal's Office*.

1993 Scholastic publishes *Picklemania*, the third sequel to *Report to the Principal's Office*.

1995 Random House publishes *Tooter Pepperday*.

1996 Random House publishes *Crash*.

1997 Scholastic publishes *The Library Card*. HarperCollins publishes *Wringer*.

1998 Random House publishes *Blue Ribbon Blues*, a sequel to *Tooter Pepperday*. Alfred A. Knopf publishes *Knots in My Yo-yo String*, Jerry Spinelli's autobiography.

2000 Knopf publishes *Stargirl*.

2002 HarperCollins publishes *Loser*.

2003 Knopf publishes *My Daddy and Me*.

Selected Reviews from *School Library Journal*

Loser
May 2002

Gr 4–6—Donald Zinkoff is a kid everyone will recognize—the one with the stupid laugh who cracks up over nothing, the klutz who trips over his own feet, the overly exuberant student who always raises his hand but never has the right answers. Following him from first grade to middle school, the story is not so much about how the boy changes, but rather how his classmates' perceptions of him evolve over the years. In first and second grades, his eccentricities and lack of coordination are accepted, but in third grade Zinkoff is "discovered." His classmates turn their critical eyes to him and brand him a loser. From then on, he endures the fate of so many outcasts—the last to be picked for the team, a favorite prey of bullies, and the butt of cruel comments from classmates. Despite his clumsiness and occasionally poor social skills, Zinkoff is a caring, sensitive boy with loving and supportive parents. He is remarkably good-natured about all the ostracizing and taunting, but his response is genuine. It is not naivete or obliviousness that gives Zinkoff his resilient spirit—he's a kid too busy being himself to worry about what other people think of him. Although perhaps not as funny as Jack Gantos's little hellion, Joey Pigza, Zinkoff is a flawed but tough kid with an unshakable optimism that readers will find endearing. "Losers" in schools everywhere will find great comfort in this story, and the kids who would so casually brand their classmates should read it, too. —Edward Sullivan, White Pine School, Tennessee

Maniac Magee
June 1990

Gr 6–10—Warning: this interesting book is a mythical story about racism. It should not be read as reality. Legend springs up about Jeffrey

"Maniac" Magee, a white boy who runs faster and hits balls farther than anyone, who lives on his own with amazing grace, and is innocent as to racial affairs. After running away from a loveless home, he encounters several families, in and around Two Mills, a town sharply divided into the black East End and the white West End. Black, feisty Amanda Beale and her family lovingly open their home to Maniac, and tough, smart-talking "Mars Bar" Thompson and other characters are all, to varying degrees, full of prejudices and unaware of their own racism. Racial epithets are sprinkled throughout the book; Mars Bar calls Maniac "fishbelly," and blacks are described by a white character as being "today's Indians." In the final, disjointed section of the book, Maniac confronts the hatred that perpetuates ignorance by bringing Mars Bar to meet the Pickwells—"the best the West End had to offer." In the feel-good ending, Mars and Maniac resolve their differences; Maniac gets a home and there is hope for at least improved racial relations. Unreal? Yes. It's a cop-out for Spinelli to have framed this story as a legend—it frees him from having to make it real, or even possible. Nevertheless, the book will stimulate thinking about racism, and it might help educate those readers who, like so many students, have no first-hand knowledge of people of other races. Pathos and compassion inform a short, relatively easy-to-read story with broad appeal, which suggests that to solve problems of racism, people must first know each other as individuals. —Joel Shoemaker, Tilford Middle School, Vinton, Iowa

Crash
1996

Gr 5–8—A winning story about seventh-grade Crash Coogan's transformation from smug jock to empathetic, mature young man. In a clever, breezy first-person style, Spinelli tackles gender roles, family relationships, and friendship with humor and feeling. As the novel opens, Crash feels passionately about many things: the violence of football; being in charge; the way he looks in shoulder pads; never being second in anything; and the most expensive sneakers at the mall. Although a stereotypical bully, the boy becomes more than one-dimensional in the context of his overworked, unavailable parents and the love he has for his grandfather, who comes to live with the Coogans and then suffers a stroke. It is because of his affection for Scooter that Crash comes to appreciate Penn Webb, a neighbor and classmate whom for years Crash has tormented and teased about his pacifism, vegetarianism, second-hand clothes, and social activism. Penn relentlessly offers friendship, which Crash finally accepts when he sees Penn's love for his own great-grandfather as a common bond. The story concludes as Penn, named by his great-grandfather for Philadelphia's famous Penn Relays, wins the school race while the elderly man looks on. Readers will devour this humorous glimpse at what jocks are made of while learning that life does not require crashing helmet-headed through it. —Connie Tyrrell Burns, Mahoney Middle School, South Portland, Maine

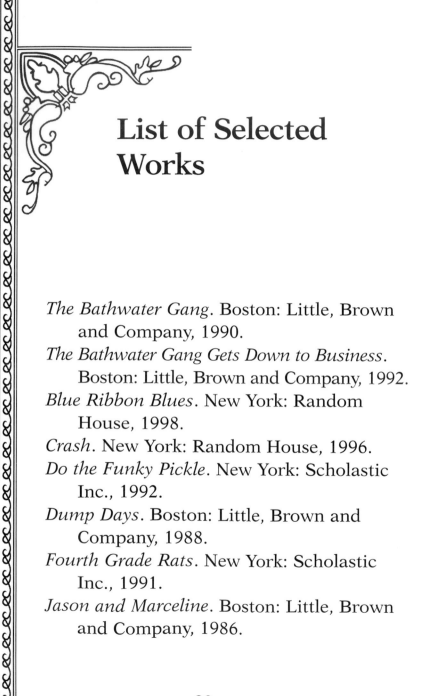

List of Selected Works

The Bathwater Gang. Boston: Little, Brown and Company, 1990.

The Bathwater Gang Gets Down to Business. Boston: Little, Brown and Company, 1992.

Blue Ribbon Blues. New York: Random House, 1998.

Crash. New York: Random House, 1996.

Do the Funky Pickle. New York: Scholastic Inc., 1992.

Dump Days. Boston: Little, Brown and Company, 1988.

Fourth Grade Rats. New York: Scholastic Inc., 1991.

Jason and Marceline. Boston: Little, Brown and Company, 1986.

Knots in My Yo-Yo String: The Autobiography of a Kid. New York: Alfred A. Knopf, 1998.

The Library Card. New York: Scholastic Inc., 1997.

Loser. New York: HarperCollins, 2002.

Maniac Magee. Boston: Little, Brown and Company, 1990.

My Daddy and Me. New York: Alfred A. Knopf, 2003.

Night of the Whale. Boston: Little, Brown and Company, 1985.

Picklemania. New York: Scholastic Inc., 1993.

Report to the Principal's Office. New York: Scholastic Inc., 1991.

Space Station Seventh Grade. Boston: Little, Brown and Company, 1982.

Stargirl. New York: Alfred A. Knopf, 2000.

There's a Girl in My Hammerlock. New York: Simon & Schuster, 1991.

Tooter Pepperday. New York: Random House, 1995.

Who Put That Hair in My Toothbrush? Boston: Little, Brown and Company, 1984.

Who Ran My Underwear Up the Flagpole? New York: Scholastic Inc., 1992.

Wringer. New York: HarperTrophy, 1997.

List of Selected Awards

***Crash* (1996)**
American Library Association Best Books
for Young Adults (1996, 1997)
School Library Journal Best Books (1996)

***Fourth Grade Rats* (1991)**
Black-Eyed Susan Award (Maryland, 1995)
South Carolina Children's Book Award
(1993)

***Maniac Magee* (1990)**
American Library Association John
Newbery Medal (1991)
Boston Globe/Horn Book Award (1990)
Pacific Northwest Library Association
Young Reader's Choice Award (1993)

Stargirl (2000)

American Library Association Best Books for
Young Adults (2001)

There's a Girl in My Hammerlock (1991)

California Young Reader Medal (1993)
New York State Reading Association Charlotte
Award (1994)

Wringer (1997)

American Library Association Newbery Honor
Book (1998)
American Library Association Notable
Children's Book (1998)
Booklist Editors' Choice Books for Youth (1997)
School Library Journal Best Books (1997)

Glossary

agent An author's representative who presents the author's books to publishers and negotiates with the publishers to get the books into bookstores and libraries.

chapter book In the book business, a book for children who read above a picture-book level, with a story complicated enough to be divided into several chapters. *The Bathwater Gang* and *Tooter Pepperday* are chapter books.

climax The emotional high point of a story, usually coming near the end.

composition In colleges and other schools, a class that teaches students to write. Spinelli taught such a class to college students.

draft   An early version of a book or story. A government program that forces young men to join the armed services.

editor   In the book business, the person at a book company responsible for working with authors.

first draft   An author's first version of a book or story.

manuscript   The text of a book that an author sends to a publisher.

material   Bits and pieces of information and ideas that a novelist can turn into a book.

middle grade   Grades four through six. Spinelli has written several books that appeal to kids in this group, including *Maniac Magee*, *Wringer*, and *Crash*.

publisher   A company that publishes books, or the person who runs the company.

rejection slip   A note that a publisher sends an author when the author sends in work that the publisher doesn't want to print.

rights   Permission to use a story or character in a particular way, like making it into a movie.

For More Information

Web Sites

Due to the changing nature of Internet links, the Rosen Publishing Group, Inc., has developed an online list of Web sites related to the subject of this book. This site is updated regularly. Please use this link to access the list:

http://www.rosenlinks.com/lab/jspi

For Further Reading

Brown, Jennifer M. "Homer on George Street." *Publishers Weekly*, July 17, 2000.

"Jerry Spinelli." *Authors and Artists for Young Adults*, Volume 41. Farmington Hills, MI: The Gale Group, 2001.

Keller, John. "Jerry Spinelli." *The Horn Book Magazine*, July/August 1991.

Kettel, Raymond P. "An Interview with Jerry Spinelli: Thoughts on Teaching Writing in the Classroom." *English Journal*, September 1994.

Murphy, Susan. "Stories That Reach the Kids: An Interview with Jerry Spinelli." *Journal of Reading*, December 1991/ January 1992.

Spinelli, Jerry. *Knots in My Yo-Yo String: The Autobiography of a Kid*. New York: Alfred A. Knopf, 1998.

Bibliography

"About the Author." *Blue Ribbon Blues*. New York: Random House, 1998.

American Library Association Web site. "The John Newbery Medal." Retrieved September 12, 2002 (http://www.ala.org/alsc/newbery_terms.html).

Cart, Michael. Review of *Loser*. *Booklist*, May 15, 2002. Reprinted on Amazon.com Web site. Retrieved September 9, 2002 (http://www.amazon.com).

Cooper, Ilene. Review of *Crash*. *Booklist*, June 1, 1996, p. 1,724.

Florence, Debbi Michiko. "An Interview with Children's Author Jerry Spinelli." JustKidInk Web site, 2002. Retrieved June 13, 2002 (http://www.geocities.com/justkidink/interviewjs.html).

Frederick, Heather Vogel. "1990 *Boston Globe/Horn Book* Awards." *The Christian Science Monitor*, November 5, 1990, p. 14.

Gale, David. Review of *Night of the Whale*. *School Library Journal*. Reprinted at Barnes and Noble Web site. Retrieved September 9, 2002 (http://search.barnesandnoble.com/booksearch).

Gallo, Don. "Jerry Spinelli." Authors 4 Teens Web site. Retrieved June 13, 2002 (http://greenwood.scbbs.com/servlet/A4Tstart?source=interview&authorid=spinelli).

Johnson, Steve. "'Maniac Magee' Is Newbery Medalist as Top Book for Kids." *Chicago Tribune*, January 15, 1991, p. 14.

Keller, John. "Jerry Spinelli." *The Horn Book Magazine*, July/August 1991.

Kerby, Mona. "Jerry Spinelli." The Author Corner Web site, April 19, 2000. Retrieved June 13, 2002 (http://www.car.lib.md.us/authco/spi-j-inf.htm).

Kirkus Reviews. Review of *Loser*. April 1, 2002, p. 499.

Kirkus Reviews. Review of *Maniac Magee*, March 15, 1990. Retrieved September 12, 2002 (http://www.kirkusreviews.com).

Knoth, Maeve Visser. Review of *Crash*. *The Horn Book Magazine*, September/October 1996, p. 600.

Lewis, Valerie. "Meet the Author: Jerry Spinelli." *Instructor*, September 1993, p. 82.

Literature Resource Center Web site. "Jerry Spinelli." Retrieved September 11, 2002 (http://galenet.galegroup.com).

Miklowitz, Gayle. "Young Adult Books: Teen-Age Love from a Male Viewpoint." *Los Angeles Times*, May 9, 1987, part 5, p. 6.

Murphy, Susan. "Stories That Reach the Kids: An Interview with Jerry Spinelli." *Journal of Reading*, December 1991/January 1992, p. 342.

Publishers Weekly. Review of *Fourth Grade Rats*. September 27, 1991, p. 58.

Publishers Weekly. Review of *Jason and Marceline*. Reprinted at Barnes and Noble Web site. Retrieved September 9, 2002 (http://search.barnesandnoble.com/booksearch).

Publishers Weekly. Review of *There's a Girl in My Hammerlock*. July 25, 1991, p. 54.

Publishers Weekly. Review of *Wringer*, June 2, 1997, p. 72.

Rausch, Tim. Review of *Wringer*. *School Library Journal*, September 1997, p. 226.

Roback, Diane, and Richard Donahue. Review of *Maniac Magee*. *Publishers Weekly*, May 11, 1990, p. 260.

Rochman, Hazel. Review of *Wringer*. *Booklist*, September 1, 1997, p. 118.

Scholastic Inc. Web site. "Jerry Spinelli's Interview Transcript." 1997. Retrieved June 3, 2002 (http://www2.scholastic.com/ teachers/authorsandbooks/authorstudies).

Sieruta, Peter D. Review of *Knots*. *The Horn Book Magazine*, January 1999, p. 87.

Sieruta, Peter D. Review of *Loser*. *The Horn Book Magazine*, July/August 2002, p. 472.

Smith, Lisa. Review of *Blue Ribbon Blues*. *School Library Journal*, May 1998, p. 126.

Spinelli, Jerry. *The Bathwater Gang*. Boston: Little, Brown, and Company, 1990.

Spinelli, Jerry. *The Bathwater Gang Gets Down to Business*. Boston: Little, Brown, and Company, 1992.

Spinelli, Jerry. *Blue Ribbon Blues*. New York: Random House, 1998.

Spinelli, Jerry. *Crash*. New York: Random House, 1996.

Spinelli, Jerry. *Do the Funky Pickle*. New York: Scholastic Inc., 1992.

Spinelli, Jerry. *Dump Days*. Boston: Little, Brown and Company, 1988.

Spinelli, Jerry. *Fourth Grade Rats*. New York: Scholastic Inc., 1991.

Spinelli, Jerry. "Interview with Jerry Spinelli," in *Stargirl*. New York: Alfred A. Knopf, 2000, p. 201.

Spinelli, Jerry. *Jason and Marceline*. Boston: Little, Brown and Company, 1986.

Spinelli, Jerry. "Jerry Spinelli." Retrieved June 13, 2002 (http://www.eyeontomorrow.com/embracingthechild/aspinelli.htm).

Spinelli, Jerry. *Knots in My Yo-Yo String: The Autobiography of a Kid*. New York: Alfred A. Knopf, 1998.

Spinelli, Jerry. *The Library Card*. New York: Scholastic Inc., 1997.

Spinelli, Jerry. *Loser*. New York: HarperCollins, 2002.

Spinelli, Jerry. *Maniac Magee*. Boston: Little, Brown and Company, 1990.

Spinelli, Jerry. Newbery Medal acceptance speech, given at the American Library Association meeting in Atlanta, Georgia, June 30, 1991.

Spinelli, Jerry. *Night of the Whale*. New York: Laurel-Leaf Books, 1985.

Spinelli, Jerry. *Picklemania*. New York: Scholastic Inc., 1993.

Spinelli, Jerry. *Report to the Principal's Office*. New York: Scholastic Inc., 1991.

Spinelli, Jerry. *Space Station Seventh Grade*. Boston: Little, Brown and Company, 1982.

Spinelli, Jerry. "Spinelli, Jerry." *Sixth Book of Junior Authors and Illustrators*. New York: H.W. Wilson, 1989. Retrieved from Educational Paperback Association Web site, June 13, 2002

(http://www.edupaperback.org/authorbios/
Spinelli_Jerry.html).

Spinelli, Jerry. *Stargirl*. New York: Alfred A.
Knopf, 2000.

Spinelli, Jerry. *There's a Girl in My Hammerlock*.
New York: Simon and Schuster, 1991.

Spinelli, Jerry. *Tooter Pepperday*. New York:
Random House, 1995.

Spinelli, Jerry. *Who Put That Hair in My
Toothbrush?* Boston: Little, Brown and
Company, 1984.

Spinelli, Jerry. *Wringer*. New York:
HarperTrophy, 1997.

Sutton, Roger. Review of *The Bathwater Gang*.
The Bulletin of the Center for Children's Books,
reprinted at Barnes and Noble Web site.
Retrieved September 9, 2002
(http://search.barnesandnoble.com/
booksearch).

Teal, Alison. Review of *Maniac Magee*. *The New
York Times Book Review*, April 21, 1993, p. 33.

Tully, Matthew. "'Maniac Magee' Author Tells
Kids He Learned a Lot from Failure."
Knight-Ridder/Tribune News Service,
April 20, 1994.

United States Navy Web site. "Naval Reserve
Force." Retrieved September 5, 2002
(http://www.navres.navy.mil/
navresfor/nrf/faq/faq_01.htm#person).

Unsworth, Robert. Review of *Jason and Marceline*. *School Library Journal*, reprinted at Barnes and Noble Web site. Retrieved September 9, 2002 (http://search.barnesandnoble.com/ booksearch).

Voice of Youth Advocates Web site. "About Us." Retrieved September 10, 2002 (http://www.voya.com/aboutus/index.shtml).

Source Notes

INTRODUCTION

1. Matthew Tully, "'Maniac Magee' Author Tells Kids He Learned a Lot from Failure," Knight-Ridder/Tribune News Service, April 20, 1994.
2. Jerry Spinelli, *Space Station Seventh Grade* (Boston: Little, Brown and Company, 1982), p. 3.

CHAPTER 1

1. Anne Johnstone, "Children's Books," *The Herald*, September 15, 2001, p. 12.
2. Jerry Spinelli, *Knots in My Yo-Yo String: The Autobiography of a Kid* (New York: Alfred A. Knopf, 1998), p. 64.
3. Kelly Milner Halls, "News for Kids Celebrity! 'Wringer' Writer Tops with Fulton County Kids," *Atlanta Constitution*, January 18, 1999, p. 7E.
4. Spinelli, *Knots in My Yo-Yo String*, p. 90.
5. Ibid.

6. Ibid., p. 89.

7. Raymond P. Kettel, "An Interview with Jerry Spinelli: Thoughts on Teaching Writing in the Classroom," *English Journal*, September 1994, p. 61.

8. Don Gallo, "Jerry Spinelli," Authors 4 Teens Web site. Retrieved June 13, 2002 (http://greenwood.scbbs.com/servlet/ A4Tstart?source=interview&authorid=spinelli).

9. Spinelli, *Knots in My Yo-Yo String*, pp. 21–22.

10. Kettel.

11. Kettel.

12. Spinelli, *Knots in My Yo-Yo String*, pp. 98–99.

13. Gallo.

14. Spinelli, *Knots in My Yo-Yo String*, p. 86.

15. Ibid., p. 106.

16. Ibid., pp. 14–15.

17. Ibid.

18. Gallo.

CHAPTER 2

1. "Transcript of Authors Live with Jerry Spinelli," Teachervision Web site, February 26, 2002. Retrieved June 13, 2002 (http://www.teachervision.com/ lesson-plans/lesson-10140.html?cb3).

2. Jerry Spinelli, *Knots in My Yo-Yo String: The Autobiography of a Kid* (New York: Alfred A. Knopf, 1998), p. 138.

3. Don Gallo, "Jerry Spinelli," Authors 4 Teens Web site. Retrieved June 13, 2002

(http://greenwood.scbbs.com/servlet/
A4Tstart?source=interview&authorid=spinelli).

4. Spinelli, *Knots in My Yo-Yo String*, p. 131.
5. Ibid., p. 12.
6. Ibid., p. 139.
7. Jerry Spinelli, "Jerry Spinelli." Retrieved June 13, 2002 (http://www.kidsreads.com/authors/au-spinelli-jerry.asp).
8. Spinelli, *Knots in My Yo-Yo String*, p. 142.
9. Ibid., pp. 143–144.
10. Raymond P. Kettel, "An Interview with Jerry Spinelli: Thoughts on Teaching Writing in the Classroom," *English Journal*, September 1994, p. 61.

CHAPTER 3

1. Jerry Spinelli, *Night of the Whale* (New York: Laurel-Leaf Books, 1985), pp. 19–20.
2. "Teacher Shares Local Author with Miquon Students," Miquon School Web site. Retrieved June 3, 2002 (http://www.miquon.org/SpinelliNews.html).
3. Don Gallo, "Jerry Spinelli," Authors 4 Teens Web site. Retrieved June 13, 2002 (http://greenwood.scbbs.com/servlet/A4Tstart?source=interview&authorid=spinelli).
4. Debbi Michiko Florence, "An Interview with Children's Author Jerry Spinelli," JustKidInk Web site, 2002. Retrieved June 13, 2002 (http://www.geocities.com/justkidink/interviewjs.html).
5. Raymond P. Kettel, "An Interview with Jerry Spinelli:

Thoughts on Teaching Writing in the Classroom," *English Journal*, September 1994, p. 61.

6. "Graduate Programs at the Writing Seminars," Johns Hopkins University Web site, 2000–2002. Retrieved September 4, 2002 (http://www.jhu.edu/~writsem/ gradprogram01.html).

7. Gallo.

8. Kettel.

9. Gallo.

10. Diana L. Winarski, "Writing: Spinelli-Style," *Teaching Pre K–8*, October 1996, p. 42.

11. Florence.

12. Gallo.

13. Winarski.

14. Jerry Spinelli, *Stargirl* (New York: Alfred A. Knopf, 2000), p. 107.

15. Pei Pei Lu, "Authors Hold Q&A on Children's Literature," *Swarthmore College Daily Gazette*, November 15, 2001. Retrieved September 2002 (http://www.sccs.swarthmore.edu/org/daily/ archive/fall_2001/therest/20011115.html).

16. Jerry Spinelli, "Jerry Spinelli." Retrieved June 13, 2002 (http://www.eyeontomorrow.com/ embracingthechild/aspinelli.htm).

17. John Keller, "Jerry Spinelli," *The Horn Book Magazine*, July/August 1991, p. 433.

18. Winarski.

19. Jerry Spinelli, "Spinelli, Jerry," *Sixth Book of Junior Authors and Illustrators* (New York: H.W. Wilson, 1989). Retrieved from Educational Paperback Association Web site June 13, 2002

(http://www.edupaperback.org/authorbios/
Spinelli_Jerry.html).

CHAPTER 4

1. Jerry Spinelli, Newbery Medal acceptance speech, given at the American Library Association meeting in Atlanta, Georgia, June 30, 1991.
2. Jerry Spinelli, *Space Station Seventh Grade* (Boston: Little, Brown and Company, 1982), p. 44.
3. Ibid., pp. 94–95.
4. John Keller, "Jerry Spinelli," *The Horn Book Magazine*, July/August 1991, p. 435.
5. Spinelli, *Space Station Seventh Grade*, pp. 24–26.
6. Keller.
7. James McPeak, review of *Space Station Seventh Grade*, *Voice of Youth Advocates*. Reprinted at Barnes and Noble Web site. Retrieved September 9, 2002 (http://search.barnesandnoble.com/booksearch).
8. *Kirkus Reviews*, review of *Space Station Seventh Grade*, November 1, 1982, pp. 1,196–1,197.
9. Amnon Rosenthal, review of *Space Station Seventh Grade*, *Bulletin for the Center for Children's Books*. Reprinted at Barnes and Noble Web site. Retrieved September 9, 2002 (http://search.barnesandnoble.com/booksearch).
10. "Author Chat," Brick Book Club Web site, 2002. Retrieved September 8, 2002 (http://www.brickbookclub.com/authorspinelli.html).
11. Scholastic Web Site, "Jerry Spinell's Interview

Transcript," 1997. Retrieved June 3, 2002 (http://www2.scholastic.com/teachers/ authorsandbooks/authorstudies).

12. Deborah Churchman, "Tales of the Awkward Age," *Washington Post*, January 13, 1985, p. 8.

13. Review of *Who Put That Hair in My Toothbrush?*, *English Journal*, March 1997, p. 103.

14. Jerry Spinelli, *Night of the Whale* (New York: Laurel-Leaf Books, 1985), p. 25.

15. David Gale, review of *Night of the Whale*, *School Library Journal*. Reprinted at Barnes and Noble Web site. Retrieved September 9, 2002 (http://search.barnesandnoble.com/booksearch).

16. Robert Unsworth, review of *Jason and Marceline*, *School Library Journal*. Reprinted at Barnes and Noble Web site. Retrieved September 9, 2002 (http://search.barnesandnoble.com/booksearch).

17. Jerry Spinelli, *Jason and Marceline* (Little, Brown and Company, 1986), pp. 200–204.

18. Gayle Miklowitz, "Young Adult Books: Teen-Age Love from a Male Viewpoint," *Los Angeles Times*, May 9, 1987, part 5, p. 6.

19. *Publishers Weekly*, review of *Jason and Marceline*. Reprinted at Barnes and Noble Web site. Retrieved September 9, 2002 (http://search.barnesandnoble.com/booksearch).

20. Unsworth.

21. *Publishers Weekly*, review of *Dump Days*. Reprinted at Barnes and Noble Web site. Retrieved September 9, 2002 (http://search.barnesandnoble.com/booksearch).

22. Roger Sutton, review of *Dump Days*, *The*

Bulletin of the Center for Children's Books. Reprinted at Barnes and Noble Web site. Retrieved September 9, 2002 (http://search.barnesandnoble.com/booksearch).

23. Susan Hepler, review of *The Bathwater Gang*, *School Library Journal*. Reprinted at Barnes and Noble Web site. Retrieved September 9, 2002 (http://search.barnesandnoble.com/booksearch).

CHAPTER 5

1. Jerry Spinelli, *Dump Days* (Boston: Little, Brown and Company, 1988), p. 36.

2. Don Gallo, "Jerry Spinelli," Authors 4 Teens Web site. Retrieved June 13, 2002 (http://greenwood.scbbs.com/servlet/ A4Tstart?source=interview&authorid=spinelli).

3. Spinelli, *Maniac Magee*, p. 2.

4. Jennifer M. Brown, "Homer on George Street," *Publishers Weekly*, July 17, 2000, p. 169.

5. Raymond P. Kettel, "An Interview with Jerry Spinelli: Thoughts on Teaching Writing in the Classroom," *English Journal*, September 1994, p. 61.

6. Mona Kerby, "Jerry Spinelli," The Author Corner Web site, April 19, 2000. Retrieved June 13, 2002 (http://www.car.lib.md.us/authco/spi-j-inf.htm).

7. Gallo.

8. *Publishers Weekly*, review of *Maniac Magee*, May 11, 1990, p. 260.

9. Alison Teal, review of *Maniac Magee*, *New York Times Book Review*, April 21, 1993, p. 33.

10. Jerry Spinelli, Newbery Medal acceptance speech, given at the American Library Association

meeting in Atlanta, Georgia, June 30, 1991.

11. Mary Blandin Bauer, "Choosing the Newbery Winner," *Washington Post*, May 12, 1991, p. x16.

12. Spinelli, Newbery Medal acceptance speech.

13. "Jerry Spinelli," Literature Resource Center Web site. Retrieved September 11, 2002 (http://galenet.galegroup.com).

14. Review of *There's a Girl in My Hammerlock*, *Publishers Weekly*, July 25, 1991, p. 54.

15. Erin Caskey, review of *There's a Girl in My Hammerlock*, *School Library Journal*, June 2000, p. 86.

16. Jerry Spinelli, *Fourth Grade Rats* (New York: Scholastic Inc., 1991), p. 1.

17. Review of *Fourth Grade Rats*, *Publishers Weekly*, September 27, 1991, p. 58.

18. Review of *Fourth Grade Rats*, *Kirkus Reviews*, 1991. Reprinted at Amazon.com Web site. Retrieved September 9, 2002 (http://www.amazon.com).

19. Pamela K. Bomboy, review of *Report to the Principal's Office*, *School Library Journal*, 1991. Reprinted at Amazon.com Web site. Retrieved September 9, 2002 (http://www.amazon.com).

20. Review of *The Bathwater Gang Gets Down to Business*, *The Horn Book*, 1993. Reprinted at Amazon.com Web site. Retrieved September 9, 2002 (http://www.amazon.com).

21. Stephanie Zvirin, review of *The Bathwater Gang Gets Down to Business*, *Booklist*. Reprinted at the Barnes and Noble Web site. Retrieved September 9, 2002

(http://search.barnesandnoble.com/booksearch).

22. Berny Morson, "Parents Gripe So Principal Pulls 42 Books; Some Say 'Young Adult' Library Was Too Heavy on the 'Adult,'" *Rocky Mountain News*, February 4, 1994, p. 4A.

23. "About the Author," *Blue Ribbon Blues* (New York: Random House, 1998), p. 73.

24. Jerry Spinelli, *Tooter Pepperday*, pp. 13–14, 25–26.

25. Mary Harris Veeder, review of *Tooter Pepperday*, *Booklist*, May 1, 1995, p. 1575.

26. *The Horn Book Magazine*, review of *Tooter Pepperday*, 1995. Reprinted at Amazon.com Web site. Retrieved September 9, 2002 (http://www.amazon.com).

27. Susan Dove Lempke, review of *Tooter Pepperday*, *Bulletin of the Center for Children's Books*. Reprinted at Barnes and Noble Web site. Retrieved September 9, 2002 (http://search.barnesandnoble.com/booksearch).

28. Ilene Cooper, review of *Crash*, *Booklist*, June 1, 1996, p. 1,724.

29. Maeve Visser Knoth, review of *Crash*, *The Horn Book Magazine*, September/October 1996, p. 600.

30. Debbi Michiko Florence, "An Interview with Children's Author Jerry Spinelli," JustKidInk Web site, 2002. Retrieved June 13, 2002 (http://www.geocities.com/justkidink/interviewjs.html).

31. *Kirkus Reviews*, review of *The Library Card*, 1997. Reprinted at Amazon.com Web site. Retrieved September 9, 2002 (http://www.amazon.com.)

32. Elsa Geskus, review of *The Library Card*,

Childhood Education, Winter 1997/1998, p. 107.

33. Jerry Spinelli, *Wringer* (New York: HarperTrophy, 1997), p. 1.
34. Ibid., pp. 3–5.
35. Wayne Martino, review of *Wringer*, *Journal of Adolescent and Adult Literacy*, December 1997/January 1998, p. 323.
36. Tim Rausch, review of *Wringer*, *School Library Journal*, September 1997, p. 226.
37. Hazel Rochman, review of *Wringer*, *Booklist*, September 1, 1997, p. 118.
38. Lisa Smith, review of *Blue Ribbon Blues*, *School Library Journal*, May 1998, p. 126.

CHAPTER 6

1. Jerry Spinelli, *Knots in My Yo-Yo String: The Autobiography of a Kid* (New York: Alfred A. Knopf, 1998), p. 148.
2. Sharon Salluzzo, review of *Knots*, *Children's Literature*. Reprinted at Amazon.com Web site. Retrieved September 9, 2002 (http://www.amazon.com.)
3. Review of *Knots in My Yo-Yo String*, *Instructor*, September 1998, p. 77.
4. Peter D. Sieruta, review of *Knots*, *The Horn Book Magazine*, January 1999, p. 87.
5. Jerry Spinelli, "Interview with Jerry Spinelli," in *Stargirl* (New York: Alfred A. Knopf, 2000), p. 201.
6. Jean Giraudoux, *Ondine*, from *Four Plays*, adapted by Maurice Valency (New York: Hill and Wang, 1958), pp. 194, 214.
7. Karen Carden, "A Bright Light in the Galaxy of

Young Adult Fiction," *Christian Science Monitor,*
December 7, 2000, p. 21.

8. Betsy Groban, review of *Stargirl, New York Times
Book Review,* September 17, 2000, p. 733.

9. Ilene Cooper, review of *Stargirl, Booklist,* June 1,
2000, p. 1883.

10. R.S., review of *Stargirl, The Horn Book
Magazine,* July 2000, p. 465.

11. Sharon Grover, review of *Stargirl, School
Library Journal,* August 2000, p. 190.

12. "Teen Scene: Anne V. Zarrow Award for Young
Readers' Literature," Tulsa City-County Library
Web site. Retrieved September 12, 2001
(http://www.tulsalibrary.com/collections/teen/
zarrow.htm).

13. Review of *Loser, Kirkus Reviews,* April 1,
2002, p. 499.

14. "An Interview with Jerry Spinelli About *Loser,*"
BookBrowse Web site, 2002. Retrieved June 13,
2002 (http://www.bookbrowse.com/dyn_/author/
authorID/455.htm).

15. Michael Cart, review of *Loser, Booklist,* May 15,
2002. Reprinted at Amazon.com Web site. Retrieved
September 9, 2002 (http://www.amazon.com).

16. Lynne F. Burke, "School Supplies—Are Stories on
Your List?" *Reading Today,* August/September
2002, p. 32.

17. Peter D. Sieruta, review of *Loser, The Horn
Book Magazine,* July/August 2002, p. 472.

18. "Author Chat," Brick Book Club Web site, 2002.
Retrieved September 12, 2002
(http://www.brickbookclub.com/authorspinelli.html).

CHAPTER 7

1. Jerry Spinelli, Newbery Medal acceptance speech, given at the American Library Association meeting in Atlanta, Georgia, June 30, 1991.
2. Raymond P. Kettel, "An Interview with Jerry Spinelli: Thoughts on Teaching Writing in the Classroom," *English Journal*, September 1994, p. 61.
3. Ibid.
4. Valerie Lewis, "Meet the Author: Jerry Spinelli," *Instructor*, September 1993, p. 82.
5. Susan Murphy, "Stories That Reach the Kids: An Interview with Jerry Spinelli," *Journal of Reading*, December 1991/January 1992, p. 343.
6. Kettel.
7. Diana L. Winarski, "Writing: Spinelli-Style," *Teaching Pre K–8*, October 1996, p. 42.
8. "Transcript of Authors Live with Jerry Spinelli." Teachervision Web site (http://www.teachervision.com).
9. Don Gallo, "Jerry Spinelli," The Author Corner Web Site, April 19, 2000. Retrieved June 13, 2002 (http://www.carrlib.md.us/authco/spi-j-infhtm).
10. Ibid.
11. Susan Shaughnessy, *Walking on Alligators: A Book of Meditations for Writers* (San Francisco: HarperSanFrancisco, 1993), p. 5.
12. Gallo.
13. Kettel.

Index

About the Author

David Seidman is an author of more than twenty books, including *Cesar Chavez: Hard Labor, U.S. Warplanes: F/A-18 Hornet, Secret Service Agents: Life Protecting the President, Civil Rights, Adam Sandler, The Young Zillionaire's Guide to Supply and Demand, Relocating to Los Angeles and Orange County, Careers in Journalism, All Gone: Things That Aren't There Anymore*, and *The Longevity Sourcebook*. He lives in West Hollywood, California.

Photo Credits

Cover courtesy of Jerry Spinelli and his family; p. 2 © M. Elaine Adams, courtesy of Jerry Spinelli.

Designer: Tahara Hasan; Editor: Annie Sommers